Julio M. Shiling

Ukraine:

A Fight for Freedom and Sovereignty

PATRIA DE MARTÍ PUBLISHING DIVISION

Miami, Florida

www.patriademarti.com

info@patriademarti.com

Printed in the United States of America

BY THE SAME AUTHOR

Dictatorships and Their Paradigms: Why Do Some Dictatorships Fall While Others Do Not?

Democratization in Cuba: A Concise Manual

11J, Exoduses, Embargo, and Martí in Cuba

Espionage, Accomplices, and Other Instruments of Castroism

China: The Monster Made in the West

Things to Know About Politics

American Exceptionalism: Creed, Culture, and Politics

Latin America Under Socialist Siege

Trump: Candidacy, Presidency, and Persecution

The Marxist Insurrection in America

The Tampered 2020 Election: Unfair and Spurious

The Biden-Obama Regime: A Fabian Path to Socialism

Ukraine: A Fight for Freedom and Sovereignty

Islamism: Enemy of Liberty

DEDICATION

For the people of Ukraine in their glorious struggle to
remain free and sovereign

ACKNOWLEDGMENT

Jose Tarano, the technical producer, and researcher of Patria de Martí, was instrumental in the coordination and preparation of this book.

CONTENTS

Preface

UKRAINE: A FIGHT FOR FREEDOM AND SOVEREIGNTY

Russia's obsession with Ukraine did not begin on February 24, 2022, when Vladimir Putin's army invaded Ukrainian territory. The intent of pulverizing the notion of Ukraine as a separate and unique cultural, historical, and anthropological entity by Russia goes as far back as to when Novgorod (part of Russia) broke away from the Kyivan Rus' in 1136. This former loose federation in Eastern and Northern Europe which was composed of East Slavic, Baltic, and Finnic peoples, is the birthplace of, both, Russia and Ukraine. While one can make the case that it is Ukraine that may have a claim of proprietorship over Russia given the Kyivan Rus' obvious hub location (in Ukraine), it has been the Russian nation that has waged an incessant battle to control her Eastern neighbor.

Upon the Bolshevik's usurpation of power in 1917, Communism's war against Ukraine exhibited greater brutality. Acts of genocide quickly followed which included politically induced famines such as the Holodomor (1929-1933), claiming the lives of 5 to 10 million Ukrainian natives. Together with Poles, Ukrainians fought the Bolsheviks bravely and attempted to keep their nations from succumbing to communist rule. Collectivization measures and the task of implementing socialism by force was imposed with more emphasis in Ukraine than in the rest of the USSR, including Russia itself.

The fall of Soviet communism did not translate into a successful transitioning to democracy for the USSR or all the former socialist bloc. Consensual government was short-lived in Russia. Since 1999, Putin has controlled political power over the Eurasian country and developed a distinct brand of kleptocracy, where former Soviet communist intelligence, military, and state enterprise managerial personnel took possession of Russia's wealth and the state. Ukraine followed the same spurious liberalization course.

The formality of Ukrainian independence in 1991, which officially granted statehood and independence to the nation of Ukraine, initiated another phase of the survival saga. From the 2004 Orange Revolution which rejected Russia's election interference, including the assassination attempt on Viktor Yushchenko, the opposition candidate who challenged Viktor Yanukovych, a Putin crony, Ukrainians fought to remain free and independent. The Kremlin puppet, Yanukovych, eventually rose to power again after promising to heed the will of Ukrainians who voted to enter European Union (EU) membership, viewing this as a safe haven from Russian imperialist ambitions.

Yanukovych reneged on his EU commitment, instead charting Ukraine on a path closer to Putin's Russia, introduced authoritarian measures, and began clamping down on the opposition. Exercising the democratic principle of the right of rebellion, Ukrainians resisted and a sequel of mass demonstrations began in November 2013 and called the Maidan Uprising. The culmination was the Revolution of Dignity (or Maidan Revolution) in February 2014. The autocratic government of Putin's man in Kyiv was toppled. A process of decommunization and the dismantling of Kremlin-regime connected Ukrainian oligarchs began.

Putin's reaction was the illegitimate invasion and subsequent annexation of Crimea (Ukrainian territory) and the fomenting of pro-Russian rebellions in Donetsk and Luhansk in March 2014, a month after the Maidan Revolution. The incursions into this Eastern region of

Ukraine, ultimately rendered the territory into a full-blown war upon the illegitimate declaration of the self-styled "Donetsk People's Republic" and the "Luhansk People's Republic." The war to recuperate this attack on Ukrainian sovereignty has been ongoing since 2014. The 2022 full-scale invasion was just a broader and bloodier operation aimed at decapitating Ukraine's state and bringing the nation back into captivity.

This book chronicles the first year of Russia's war on Ukraine through essays and articles. Ukrainian resistance has been epic. This battle between tyranny and freedom must be examined comprehensively. The West has reluctantly aided Ukraine. The Free World's help, however, appears to be targeted enough for the Ukrainian forces not to collapse but not sufficient to defeat the Russian invaders. The fact that Ukraine is still free and independent is of enormous importance. It is seminal that this heroic story be told and remembered.

1 Here's Why Russia Bullies the U.S.

The doddering Biden-Harris administration, frail and without a moral compass, appears to be no match for the Russian despot.

The Biden-Harris administration celebrated its one-year anniversary, embarrassed and defeated. Its project to bring socialism to the U. S. has so far failed. Both, in the popular front by the non-elitist, non-woke, traditionalist American society (the majority) and in Congress, the Left is witnessing an adamant resistance. The inflation rate is the highest in nearly four decades. Its one-dimensional, unscientific COVID policy is a disgrace. The missed liberation opportunity in Cuba, and the collapse of Afghanistan demonstrate that American resolve, under this presidency, is infirm. Russia has added to the country's woes and is now bullying America.

Despite denying that an invasion of Ukraine is imminent, Vladimir Putin has amassed over 100,000 Russian troops on the sovereign country's border. In 2014, confronting the flimsy leadership of another Democratic president (Barack Obama), Russia transgressed Ukrainian territory and stole Crimea. Putin has been making the same arguments about the Russian minority in Ukraine that Adolf Hitler made about ethnic Germans in the Sudetenland and Austria when Germany invaded and seized those territories. Had Hitler not had a weak counterpart like Neville Chamberlain, history may have taken a different course. Likewise, Putin is acting on his perceptions of the Biden-Harris leadership formula.

Russia's autocrat is a lawyer and was a KGB intelligence officer for fifteen years (1975-1990) who retired with the rank of lieutenant colonel. In 1998, Putin returned to the intelligence field to head the Federal Security Service, the KGB's successor espionage and counterespionage agency. Like the short-lived Russian democratic experience of the early 20th century (1905-1917), the fall of Soviet communism in 1991 saw democracy's death begin to take shape when Putin was appointed prime minister in 1999 and later elected president in 2000. Instead of the General Secretary of the Communist Party position, an elected Czar, in questionable elections, is more characteristic of Putin's current role. Yet, Russian hegemonic expansion around the globe is a goal of post-Soviet Russia's authoritarian regime.

Russian deputy foreign minister Sergei Ryabkov hinted on Thursday, January 13 that Russia could deploy military infrastructure, troops, and/or missiles, to Cuba and Venezuela. The fact is that Russian incursion in the Western Hemisphere has been an ongoing phenomenon since 2000. An elaborate spying satellite called Glonass was set up by Putin's Russia in Nicaragua in 2016. While the Obama-Castro pact was publicly unfolding during the former president's visit to Cuba in 2016, a Russian spy submarine lay in Havana Harbor just blocks from where the American delegation was meeting.

The Havana Syndrome, that neurological malady from probable high-density microwave radiation because of suspected cyber espionage, has inflicted irreversible harm to at least one hundred and thirty American diplomats and their families around the world. The Putin regime is believed to be the mastermind behind this heinous causal instrument of espionage and warfare. The Russian Tupolev Tu-160 bombers with the capability of carrying nuclear weaponry were dispatched to Venezuela, in 2018, in a show of solidarity with the Maduro dictatorship. It is no secret that Putin has been a consistent supplier of armaments, for over a decade, to the socialist regime in Caracas. Among the first two international figures to congratulate the Cuban communist regime on its crackdown of the 11th of July Uprising were the dictators of China, Xi Jinping, and Russia.

Putin has upped the ante, given the current American government's inertia in defending freedom. The Russian regime stated on January 21that it wants all NATO troops to vacate Bulgaria and Romania. Putin is trying to redraw the world map to pre-1997. Undoubtedly, the imperialistic demands by the Russian dictator will continue their escalation mode. Historically, Russian despotic regimes have advanced when weakness if perceived by their American counterpart. John F. Kennedy's betrayal at the Bay of Pigs liberation attempt in Cuba, in April 1961, proved pivotal in Nikita Khrushchev's calculations. Four months later the Berlin Wall was erected and the placement of nuclear missiles on the imprisoned island was calibrated.

The doddering Biden-Harris administration, frail and without a moral compass, appears to be no match for the Russian despot. The question becomes, not how determined the current American executive branch will go in supporting liberty and confronting tyranny, but rather how bold is tyranny feeling these days.

2 The Free World Has Betrayed Ukraine

If Kyiv falls, a guerrilla war must ensue, and the Free World must support the brave Ukrainian people with logistics and weaponry.

It is now official. The Free World has betrayed Ukraine. The Left and some on the Right, harbored faith that the Putin regime would succumb to the West's rhetoric, which has demonstrated itself cynically naive. President Joe Biden's speech and subsequent press conference of February 24 sounded more like a reporter briefing the public on the news that the supposed leader of the world's greatest democracy. It was clear months before, that the decision to violate Ukraine's sovereignty and international law, was contingent on how weak the Russian dictator viewed the American president as being.

Putin's rationale for forcefully incorporating Ukraine into the 21st century version of the Union of Soviet Socialist Republics is deliriously Hitlerian. The *Lebensraum* ("living space") argument was as invalid for the National Socialist dictator, as it is for his Russian counterpart. The Kremlin's war manifestation was out laid by Putin in his July 12, 2021, article "On the Historical

Unity of Russian and Ukrainians." "Russians and Ukrainians were one people," wrote the Russian tyrant. However, the facts reveal they are not.

The Kyivan Rus' was a federation of Slavic, Baltic, and Finnic tribes that was formed in the ninth century and encompassed Eastern and Northern Europe, including modern-day Ukraine and Russia. It terminated with the Mongol invasion in the 1240s. Putin's abstract claim to Ukraine rests on the false narrative that springs from that reading of history. Ukrainians, however, could make the same argument, but in reverse. In other words, they could claim that Russia belongs to Ukraine. The Kyivan Rus', after all, was based out of Kyiv. The fact is that both countries share common traits as do Latin Americans, Asians, Africans, and Europeans. But Russia and Ukraine are distinctly different, culturally and anthropologically. Their difference now is even more astounding. One is a democracy and the other a dictatorship.

It is on the systemic and moral distinctions between the two opposing models of governance and the action of Putin's Russia against Ukraine, that the Free World has shamed itself. Additionally, by not having acted swiftly to aid the freely elected and legitimate government of President

Volodymyr Zelensky when a Russian invasion was imminent, the West has invited tyrannical aggression around the globe form other wicked regimes in China, Iran, North Korea, Cuba, and other Western Hemispheric socialist satellites.

The reaction by the United States has been pathetic. The actions being levied against the Putin regime and labeled as "sanctions" are an insult to the intelligence of Americans, Ukrainians, and free citizens of the world. The Biden measures clearly avoid penalizing Russian oil exports. When one considers that oil and natural gas are Russia's main source of hard-currency entry, an exemption of this type only assures Putin that his dictatorship will continue to have the resources to rage war and genocide.

Not modulating the Society for Worldwide Interbank Financial Telecommunication system (SWIFT) to exclude Russian transactions, displays further gross negligence on the part of the Biden administration. This measure would severely limit the Kremlin's access to money. Another important step would be to stop putting petrodollars in Putin's pockets. Incredibly as it may seem, still as of this moment, the United States is buying oil from the former KGB officer's regime. According to the U.S. Energy

Information Administration, in 2021 Russia was America's third-largest supplier of oil. Any serious consideration of non-military assistance to freedom's noble cause in Ukraine, must include SWIFT system blocking of all Russian transactions and an immediate cease of purchasing Putin's oil.

Ukraine possessed one-third of the former USSR's nuclear arsenal. It conditionally turned in the nuclear weapons in 1994, with assurances from the United States, United Kingdom, and the Russian Federation (while it was still a democracy). The Budapest Memorandum, signed under the auspice of the United Nations (UN), assured Ukraine that its denuclearization would receive the guarantee by the three signatories and that they would "refrain from the threat or use of force against the territorial integrity or political independence of Ukraine, and that none of their weapons will ever be used against Ukraine except in self-defense or otherwise in accordance with the Charter of the United Nations." The cited agreement further stipulated that the UN would respond if Ukraine ever became "the victim of an act of aggression."

Putin's twenty-two-year dictatorship, from day one, charted the course of the recuperation of a less-ideologized version of Soviet socialism, albeit with modifications to its economic model. The 2008 invasion of Georgia, followed by the 2014 heist of Crimea, should have alerted the United States to the Russian despot's nature and intentions. The Minsk agreements "settling" the Crimea invasion was violated from the onset, following the Soviet precedent of violating all signed agreements with the West. Since 2014, Putin unleashed a guerrilla war against Ukraine in the regions he calls today "peoples republics."

The Free World should have been present in Ukraine, as surely the Zelensky government would have welcomed an armed American and British presence. The Budapest Memorandum was enough justification. No need for NATO. Now what must be done, in addition to real economic sanctions, is military hardware for the Ukrainian defenses. If Kyiv falls, a guerrilla war must ensue, and the Free World must support the brave Ukrainian people with logistics and weaponry. If all these actions are diligently followed, Putin could be toppled. That should be the longer-term goal. Ending the Putin regime means saving Ukraine, Russia, and subsequently, Belarus. That is a worthy objective.

3 Ukraine's Lessons for Captive Nations

Civilians across the world must pay attention and learn from Ukrainians' bravely pushback against Russia's savage military assault.

Less than a week has passed since Vladimir Putin launched its brutal blitzkrieg offensive to take over Ukraine. There is a reason why the glorious Ukrainian flag still flies in Kyiv and other major cities in that country of heroes. Most media pundits, democratic governments, socialist accomplices, and academics had little hope that the sovereign government of Volodymyr Zelensky would survive. The military power, truth be told, made betting on an early Russian victory a more plausible bet. No one expected this war of David and Goliath to have lasted so long. Captive nations like Cuba, Venezuela, Nicaragua, Iran, and Bolivia (to name a few) can learn a lot from Ukraine's resistance experience. Here are six points that freedom fighters around the globe should take note of.

Lesson # 1 Pacifism and Civil Disobedience Have Severe Limits

In republics with consensual systems of government, civil disobedience is a remarkable weapon to provoke political change. Free and fair elections also facilitate valid modes of civic expression and civil society activism. In tyrannical regimes—especially of the totalitarian type—actions of civil disobedience and peaceful protests which are unaccompanied with actual or potential belligerent deportment, usually yield little results of systemic change.

Soviet communism fell, along with its socialist-block European satellites because there was a Cold War that got much warmer when the Reagan Administration ditched containment and reverted to a state policy of rolling back socialism. Ukrainians are combating the enemy with lethal arms and not protest signs.

Lesson # 2 The Importance of the Second Amendment in the U.S.

If anyone doubts the importance of the American constitutional notion for "A well-regulated Militia, being necessary to the security of a free State, the right of the people to keep and bear Arms," Ukraine is a stern example. Tyrants like an unarmed citizenry. Monopolizing weapons only for political actors in power is a huge mistake. Republican self-government schemes work best when those that govern have something to fear of the governed.

Lesson # 3 Sanctions Work When Comprehensively Applied

Do not believe the moral relativists, commercial vultures, or utopian laissez-faire radicals, when they tell you that sanctions do not work. They definitely do—when applied consistently and in an integrated manner. The end of South Africa's apartheid can best be explained by the thorough international campaign to isolate the racist government.

The American embargo on the Cuban communist regime is an example of a sound moral policy in which politicians have weakened it throughout the years, denying its full potential for success. The fact that the U.S. has not materially internationalized the sanctions against the island's Marxist dictatorship is another reason why it has not had the impact that it could. What the democratic world is doing to the Putin regime is a step in the right direction. It needs only to intensify the strategy.

Lesson # 4 Engagement-Type, "Reset" Policies Do Not Work with Tyrants

Former President Barack Obama, from day one of his presidency, made his mea culpa doctrine the official mantra of his foreign policy. America's worst enemies—

namely Iran, Cuba, China, North Korea, and Russia—according to the Obama foreign policy, were antagonistic because of the United States' perceived superiority complex (Obama rejects American exceptionalism) and its "aggressive" behavior. With the Putin regime, Obama announced its "reset" in 2009, by way of then-Secretary of State Hillary Clinton, in an awkward and cartoonish ceremony where Russian Foreign Minister Sergei Lavrov was presented with a red "reset button" representing the false perception of improved ties.

Putin enjoyed a bonanza of international power consolidation under Obama's watch. The 2009 decision to scrap Europe's missile defense shield program, which was underway since 2007, left Europe unprotected. The Syrian "red line" bluff statement, served to aggrandize Russian imperial activism with its rescue of the Assad dictatorship, in partnership with Iran in 2012. The criminal annexation of Crimea and the failed Minsk agreements (2014), which sought to stop Russian expansion in the Ukrainian regions of Donetsk and Luhansk, were mockingly violated from the onset. Russia's 2011 entry into the World Trade Organization was facilitated by the 44th president. Obama embodied an "engagement" approach to Russian tyranny.

It failed, as have all détente-like policies with the regimes of Russia, Cuba, China, and Iran.

Lesson # 5 The Myth of Immutability

Monsters tend to build myths around themselves. Putin, like his Soviet predecessors, formulated a false image of strength, competency, and invincibility. Politicians like Obama and Germany's Angela Merkel helped project this fallacy with their appositeness postures. Ukraine has, so far, demonstrated that Putin's Russia is a paper tiger, as Mao once quipped about the United States. This does not mean that it is not a killing machine. The fact that Ukrainians have effectively frustrated what many thought would be a walk in the park and managed to levy great pain to Russians in the battleground testifies to the power of right makes might and heroism is a game-changer.

Lesson # 6 Courageous Leadership Inspires a Valiant Citizenry

Zelensky is the 21st-century embodiment of Winston Churchill. Curiously, Putin is a cross between Adolf Hitler on his Lebensraum diatribe and Joseph Stalin on nationalism ("socialism in one country"). The enormous sacrifice being exercised by Ukrainians in the defense of their fatherland has been stimulated greatly by the nation's leadership. Weakness, cowardice, and vacillation only invite aggression from your enemies. Ukraine's resistance and determination to be free and independent is not contingent on whether Putin captures Kyiv or not. The heroic fight will go on. A war of liberation will ensue.

Ukraine has done much to elevate the democratic ethos. It has reminded us of the need for heroism, and armed campaigns searching for freedom. Bullies are predatory and thrive on weakness and limited endeavors of defense. Captive nations can and must learn from what is happening in Eastern Europe. Thank you, Ukraine! We stand with you!

4 What Military Help Must America Now Give Ukraine?

Cowardice only fosters aggression from your enemies.

The Russian invasion of Ukraine has borne out an ensemble of World War II characters. Volodymyr Zelensky is impressively Churchillian. Vladimir Putin is staunchly Hitlerian. Joe Biden is Neville Chamberlain, pure and simple. The preemptive blunders made by the Free World that potentially could have averted Putin's latest territorial overreach, enter the realm of a betrayal. Complying with the 1994 Budapest Memorandum, committed the United States and the United Kingdom with defending Ukraine's sovereignty. At this point, what must America do now to help Ukraine?

There are a series of measures which the United States could do. These actions should remain in effect whether Ukraine loses its independence and is occupied by Russia. In other words, should the Putin regime cause the collapse of the free Ukrainian state, a resistance insurgency will likely spring forth. This effectual government in arms, de facto and de jure, will become the legitimate voice of Ukraine. America must continue aiding Ukrainians and maintain this comprehensive policy until Ukraine is free once again. American military aid must flow now to the embattled Eastern European country. This must include tactical and logistical assistance.

Air superiority will likely weigh in favor of the victor. The reason Putin is attacking with missiles fired from a distance instead of air force bombers, is because of the success of Ukrainian antiaircraft weaponry. Additionally, Ukraine still has planes that they have performed well against Russian aircraft. America must accelerate and amplify its transfer of military hardware to Ukrainians.

Why hasn't the United States delivered A-10 Thunderbolt airplanes to Ukraine already? The 40-mile caravan of Russian armored battalions preparing to advance on Kyiv have been sitting idly and visibly for days. They are an easy target which would give Ukraine a big military score. The A-10 Thunderbolt aircraft is especially formulated for that task. The Ukrainian Air Force has qualified pilots who have been trained to fly them.

Stinger surface-to-air missiles would go along way in neutralizing Putin's air power. America must step up their delivery to the Ukrainian military forces. Promised delivery of MIG-29 fighter jets by Poland, Bulgaria, and Slovakia for Ukraine after stalling, now appears to have died. Politico reported on Friday, March 4, that the idea of badly needed fighter jets to help Ukrainians push back on the Russian invaders has been scrapped. The bizarre change of mind and arguably treacherous act by the European Union democracies, appears to have been pressured by NATO appeasement postures. Polish President Andrzej Duda, with NATO Secretary-General Jens Stoltenberg at his side, stated on Tuesday, March 1, at Łask Air Base in Poland, that sending jets "would open a military interference in the Ukrainian conflict."

The Russian dictator's "nuclear" option threat has paid off for him. The West, with NATO being its emblematic post-World War II military command center, craved in and abandoned Ukraine (once again). America must not follow suit in allowing the Putin regime to have a monopoly of air power command over Ukrainian territory. If the Biden-Harris administration continues its Chamberlain course, the Russian führer will again threaten with "nuclear" talk. Who's next? Poland, Estonia, Latvia, or Finland? Cowardice only fosters aggression from your enemies. Helping Ukrainians successfully fight the Russians today, could spare Americans having to do it tomorrow.

5 Combating Putin Can Promote Freedom in the Americas

The Putin regime, upon its consolidation, immediately sought to reestablish its presence in the Western Hemisphere.

The resolve by the West to challenge Vladimir Putin's Leninist war against Ukraine and consequently, the democratic order, appears to be gaining momentum. The will and determination of Ukraine's president, Volodymyr Zelensky, and its valiant people to remain free and independent, has pushed the Free World into getting more proactive in its solidarity with the besieged nation, albeit painfully slow. The results from this epic shift in moral positioning and strategic engagement by the world's democracies has for years been indifferent and wimpish. Now there are attractive opportunities for liberation processes to unfold in socialist dictatorial regimes in the Americas.

On Tuesday, March 8, President Joe Biden announced that the United States was "banning all imports of Russian oil and gas energy." The United Kingdom's Business Secretary Kwasi Kwarteng also declared on the same day that his country would "phase out imports of Russian oil in response to Vladimir Putin's illegal invasion of Ukraine by the end of the year." Poland added to the day's big news when it reversed course and agreed to supply Ukraine with M-29 Soviet-era fighter jets. The Polish Ministry of Foreign Affairs stated that they could be provided "immediately and free of charge."

Putin's rise to power was significant in not just burying the nascent Russian democracy. It signaled a slow return to the former Soviet Union's imperialistic overtures. This has been specifically the case in Latin America. Cuban communism, a formidable agent and operating base for international socialism at the service of the USSR from its onset, developed a parasitic dependency on Soviet subsidies at the tune of $2 billion annually. When the Kremlin's 6,000 combat troops stationed in Cuba left in 1991, the relationship entered a comatose phase. It all began to change with Putin from 2000.

The Castro communist regime and its socialist satellites, particularly Venezuela and Nicaragua, share a symbiotic relationship. The fall of Soviet communism produced a new continental dictatorial model, which was developed in

1990 at the Sao Paulo Forum, of which Havana is its architect and overseer, and Venezuela its principal financier. Putin's autocratic reconstruction of post-Soviet Russia shares many characteristics with the Castro-invented Sao Paulo Forum despotic prototype: rigged voting schemes which include an irrelevant and powerless "opposition"; a mixed economy with crony and state capitalist partners; brutal repression and state terror as policy; no rule of law; and a less-ideologically pronounced political discourse. Venezuela, Nicaragua, and Bolivia are clear examples in Latin America of this despotic model.

The Putin regime, upon its consolidation, immediately sought to reestablish its presence in the Western Hemisphere. The preeminent role that the Castro dictatorship has played in communism's post-Soviet mutation, assured Havana that Russia would be interested in collaborating with its historical subversive partner in the continent. Intelligence collaboration between the two tyrannical regimes and Castroism's protégés, was a given. The 2017 opening of a mammoth Russian electronic intelligence-gathering facility near Managua, part of Putin's Glonass GPS spy network, was consistent with the alliance that had been reforged.

Putin's Russia has been especially diligent in its cyberespionage operations. The Havana Syndrome, the suspected malady side effect of high-intensity microwave radiation used for distance espionage, and which has inflicted hundreds of American diplomats and their families, has the fingerprints of the former KGB spymaster's regime. The presence of the Russian spy ship Viktor Leonov CCB-175, anchored blocks away from where the American delegation was staying as the 2015 diplomatic reestablishment talks between the Obama administration and the Castro regime were going on, made evident that Putinism was a filtered down version of the Soviet hegemonic mode of operation.

In 2014, Putin "forgave" Castro communism's $30 billion Soviet-era debt. Unfazed by the Cuban Marxist dictatorship's delinquent borrower history, Russia extended to the island granted loans totaling $2.3 billion, between 2009 and 2019. Putin's puppet legislative body, the Duma, recently deferred the Castro regime's payment of said debt until 2027, given its stated inability to pay. In other words, Russia has continued its finance of the Americas' continental socialism.

The Russian financial system serves communist Cuba, Venezuela, and Nicaragua as a mechanism for avoiding American sanctions. Putin's banks have been used to make payments abroad, for example, by Maduro regime enterprises to European companies, after the Trump administration imposed sanctions on the Venezuelan dictatorship. It is also likely, additionally, that they are used for laundering money from drug trafficking, a profitable business for Marxist regimes and movements in the Western Hemisphere.

The American decision to bar 13 of Russia's main banks from having access to the Swift network, which is commonly used between financial institutions for international transactions, will impact adversely the continent's socialist regimes. Juan González, National Security Council Senior Director for Western Hemisphere Affairs (NSC) for the Biden administration, stated, "The sanctions on Russia are so robust that they will have an impact on those governments that have economic affiliations with Russia." The Colombian-born NSC official who formerly worked for the Obama administration, added, "So Venezuela is going to start to feel that pressure, Nicaragua is going to start to feel that pressure, just like Cuba."

The United States and the Free World has a golden opportunity to "kill two (or more) birds with one stone." Considering that the "birds" in question are the ruthless tyrannic regimes in Cuba, Venezuela, Nicaragua, and Bolivia (potentially), the war to help Ukraine, can also help foster freedom here in the Americas. The Biden administration has the unique opportunity to do what is right. Stopping Putin in Europe could yield some wonderful dividends for the enslaved peoples of the Western Hemisphere.

6 Fear of War Will Cause a Bigger and Bloodier Conflict

Putin is losing this senseless war he started. According to Russian accounts, it should have been over in a few days. It wasn't.

History serves many purposes, among them the knowledge that can be gained by studying and applying its lessons. War is one of those issues where politicians often ignore history, choosing instead to indulge in psychoanalytic historiography. The world's democratic leaders, starting with President Joe Biden, are crafting national security decisions based on studying the pattern of thoughts, feelings, and behavior of the enemies of freedom. Fearing to go to war may precisely end up provoking a new one.

John F. Kennedy changed, at the last moment, the most seminal component of the structured plan of more than a year for an expedition of Cuban exiles to initiate a belligerent liberation campaign. This was to be carried out in coordination with an already active opposition force fighting on various fronts on the island. The Massachusetts Democrat, a darling of the U.S. soft left, dismissed the vital air support on which the plan was based, among other strategic elements. Kennedy's fear of appearing "imperialist" and thus provoking a possible Soviet reaction, not only consolidated Castro's communist dictatorship but also emboldened the USSR.

In less than four months, Nikita Khrushchev surrounded the free part of Berlin with a wall. The intention was to isolate West Berlin and force its capitulation. Within a year and three months, the dictators of Cuba and the Soviet Union signed a secret agreement to install offensive nuclear missiles aimed at U.S. cities ninety miles from their shores. Latin America has been the theater of a never-ending Cold War with socialism since the Prince of Camelot betrayed the Cubans in 1961 having the idea in mind of avoiding war.

The Bolshevik coup d'état of 1917 dislodged the short-lived Russian democracy. When the Russians went to war to fight the Bolsheviks who had seized power, a brutal civil war ensued between the "Whites" (anti-Communists) and the "Reds" (Communists) from 1917 to 1922. The free world, at first, took part to help the Russians fight communism. However, Western support was lukewarm, lackluster—ultimately, they abandoned the White Army allies who challenged the Leninist regime. Woodrow

Wilson, the American president of the day, opposed a relevant military campaign to combat communism, naively claiming that doing so would "add to the present sad turmoil in Russia rather than cure it."

Franklin Delano Roosevelt's benign opinion of Joseph Stalin, which led him to allow socialism to swallow Central and Eastern Europe, is another example of presidential myopia that has left brutal scars on humanity. Wilsonian logic, like that of Kennedy and Roosevelt, will remain a stain on American leadership. Over one hundred million deaths are, credibly, attributable to communism. Neville Chamberlain's underlying thesis of "peace" at all costs and his false reading of Adolf Hitler followed a familiar pattern of weakness that blatant dictators and their regimes exploit.

These are just a few poignant examples, in which the common denominator is that all were based on a misunderstanding of the nature of the enemies of freedom and an underlying fear of war or its escalation. These gross misinterpretations and their subsequent failed policies not only failed to prevent severe human pain and suffering but encouraged a bold attitude on the part of despots who were willing to test the resolve of their perceived weak democratic counterparts. War flared up.

Ukraine, a sovereign and free state, was attacked by a foreign and autocratic regime. Any argument of "established spheres of influence" to explain Russian aggression rests entirely on illegitimate acts. If Vladimir Putin's invasion were rationally justified or correct, as some realpolitik fundamentalists argue, then the independence of a sovereign nation like Ukraine is illegitimate. Since there is no moral or legal basis for this madness, then clearly Putin is a global bully who must be stopped. When you take into account the genocide that is now occurring, something the Russian dictator's Soviet predecessors taught him all too well on how to do, it becomes imperative that the Free World acts decisively.

Kyiv is under siege. If Putin's armed forces blockade the city and attempt to strangle it, just as Khrushchev did in 1961 with Berlin, the West will have no choice but to initiate airlift to prevent starvation and freezing of the brave citizens of the Ukrainian capital. Why continue to dodge what must be done? Immediately send President Volodymyr Zelensky the MIG-29 fighter planes, which Poland has already agreed to provide. In addition, deliver to the Ukrainian Armed Forces powerful anti-aircraft equipment. Among the most effective are the THAAD (Terminal High Altitude Area Defense) anti-ballistic missile defense system, the Patriot (MIM-104) and the MEADS (Medium Extended Air Defense System) air and missile defense mechanisms.

It is necessary to establish a humanitarian no-fly zone over Ukraine to prevent civilian deaths. This limited option would ensure safe passage for non-combatants. Concern that the war may escalate due to the creation of a demilitarized air zone ignores the fact that Russian tactics are increasingly horrific. We are seeing a strategic replication of Syria and Chechnya.

Putin is losing this senseless war he started. According to Russian accounts, it should all be over in a few days. It hasn't. This is because the Ukrainian people are fighting with a purpose. They are not giving up. The West has helped, reluctantly, at a snail's pace and with a shaky hand. However, it is Putin who should be trembling. The fact that he is asking the Syrians and the Chinese for help tells us that the Russian dictator understands the limits of his resources. Biden and the free world must stop being reactive and become proactive.

Zelensky's mentor, Winston Churchill, described it brilliantly. "You were given a choice between dishonor and war. You chose dishonor and you will have war." Hopefully, the West will wake up in time to avoid repeating the mistakes of the past.

7 Debunking Russia's Lies

Some of the lies told by Russia are doing a great disservice to freedom, republicanism, and the Russian people themselves.

There are a vast number of false narratives involving Ukraine and Russia, within the context of the latter's invasion of the former. These bogus claims are not coming exclusively from dictator Vladimir Putin's propaganda news outlets and spokespersons. Some individuals on both the left and the right are echoing these questionable claims. Considering all that is at stake, it is paramount to set things clear and debunk the main falsehoods made by the Putin regime, by those pushing his propaganda, or some well-intentioned thinkers that are framing their arguments on inaccurate premises.

Lie # 1 "Ukraine Is under Russia's Sphere of Influence"

The notion that Russia is entitled to exercise discretionary authority over Ukrainian affairs is illegitimate. Ukraine is a free and sovereign nation with a consensual system of governance. The Ukrainian people get to decide, by way of their elected officials, the policies that their country adopts.

If one is to accept as valid that Russia has a rational basis for its claim of Lebensraum ("living space"), then Nazi Germany was correct in its forced absorption of parts of the Czech Republic in 1938 and other parts of Europe. (More on this topic in a forthcoming article).

Lie # 2 The Revolution of Dignity (or Maidan Revolution) Was a "Coup""

The Revolution of Dignity, that popular uprising where the Ukrainian people successfully removed from power an autocratic Russian stooge, is consistent with the democratic sacrosanct principle of the Right of Revolution. Free people have a duty, as well as their right, to rebel against tyrannical authority and overthrow that government, when its actions betray the basis of their original intent to rule. In other words, if a government is elected democratically but in its execution of power abandons the parameters of its social pact and rules unjustly, they cease to be a democratic government.

The U.S. Declaration of Independence (1776), the Declaration of the Rights of Man and of the Citizen (1789), and the U.N. Universal Declaration of Human Rights (1948) are some legal and moral instruments that embrace the Right of Revolution. A coup, on the other hand, is an illegal act that involves the forced removal of a legitimate government that has remained faithful to its limited role, temporarily granted to it, by a free citizenry. Viktor Yanukovych violated his authority when he suppressed dissent, curtailed civil liberties, passed draconian censorship laws, and aligned Ukraine with Russian interests. This was a cardinal betrayal, since the fundamental premise of his political campaign was to seek proximity with Europe, Putin's nemesis. (More on this topic in a forthcoming article).

Lie # 3 Ukraine Has Always Been Part of Russia

The "unity" began in 882 with the Kyivan Rus'. The loose federation of people and tribes from Eastern and Northern Europe which lasted until the 1240s, when the Mongols invaded, is the basis of this Russian folkloric historiography. It is a curious fact that Kyiv (in Ukraine, not in Russia) was the capital of this federation. The truth is that after that, Ukraine was occupied by differing foreign entities throughout most of its history. Despite this, it managed to anthropologically develop its own idiosyncratic identity, culture, and language.

Soviet communism, since its beginning with the Bolshevik coup in 1917, waged an incessant war to control and dominate Ukraine. The Putin regime, a loyal heir to communist tyranny, has done everything in his power to wrestle Ukraine back to its captive colony status. The timing of the previous (2014) and the present invasion of Ukrainian territory, for the former KGB spymaster, has depended on his perceived weakness of American leadership and nothing else.

Lie # 4 Putin Invaded Because of "Neutrality" Violations on the Part of Ukraine

When the Russian dictator invaded and annexed Crimea and installed a Russian insurgency in Donetsk and Luhansk in 2014, Ukraine was technically "neutral." When the Putin regime recently skewed his pseudo- "people's republic" scheme of the other two regions where Russian-backed separatists waged an eight-year guerrilla war, Ukraine was neutral. "Neutrality" for Russia means Ukrainian submission and its colonial rule.

Lie # 5 Ukraine Must Be Demilitarized

In 1994, Ukraine had the world's third-largest nuclear inventory. In that year, Ukraine made one of its biggest mistakes. It voluntarily gave up the entirety of its nuclear weapons. That is what the Budapest Memorandum, a U.N.

facilitated document, was about. Ukraine believed in the commitment that its guarantors, the United States and United Kingdom, would honor the 1994 agreement's solemn assurance that Ukraine's sovereignty would be respected and defended. There should be no doubt that Ukrainians regret greatly having ceded those weapons. Putin would not have invaded.

Lie # 6 Putin Fights Cultural Marxism; Therefore, He Is Conservative, Anti-globalist, and Anticommunist

The premise that Putin is conservative, anti-globalist, and anti-communist is false. Yes, the Russian autocrat fights the venom of gender ideology, transgenderism, radical feminism, and other plans of political action that get their rationalization from cultural Marxism's critical theory arsenal. The fact is; however, communist China and Islamic Iran also combat vehemently all of those same Neo-Marxist tenets. Cultural Marxism is a mode of subversion in Western democracies. Once political power is reached, the communist (China), post-communist (Putinism), and Islamism (Iran) crush any vestige that questions its absolutism.

Putin has actively sought to reinsert Russia in the world where the USSR left off, albeit with a 21st-century revision of its production relations and economic model. Russia's state-sponsored oligarchs, all Putin made, are globalists by definition. This is the case of Putin himself. Autarky, a policy of national self-sufficiency, is antithetical to, both the Soviet Union and Putin's praxis. The Russian dependency on oil exports to finance the country's basic needs exemplifies this. Russia's intimate, intertwining relationship with the Western Hemisphere's socialist dictatorships is one example of its globalist worldview.

The nonsensical arguments being put out by some who should better, do a great disservice to freedom and the republican system. The Putin regime is a product of Soviet communism. It is carrying out a version of the Holodomor. Ukraine is democracy's battlefield today.

8 In Defense of a No-Fly Zone in Ukraine

Many have rushed to argue against a no-fly zone, but with the right military equipment from the U.S. and NATO, Ukraine could discourage Putin's missiles and planes from flying over his country for war and genocide purposes.

As the free and sovereign nation of Ukraine battles the invading second most powerful army in the world, the West continues to evade its responsibility. Dictator Vladimir Putin has launched his captive nation into a war against the international democratic order. To believe that Russia's imperial quest will stop at Ukraine's borders is an exercise of supreme naivety. The West is in denial if it believes it is not currently under attack. Here are some reasons why implementing a no-fly zone of some sort over Ukraine makes sense.

Call it World War III or IV (if one counts the Cold War as a world war), the truth is that aggression from pillars of evil has been in a constant war against the free world. One example is communist China's asymmetrical warfare since 1978. Another has been the installation of the Putin regime in 2000. It launched another front against free societies, a post-Soviet version. Authoritarian Russia took a mixed combat approach that has been, both, asymmetrical (cyber-attacks, espionage, economic, foreign interference) and traditional (Chechnya, Moldavia, Syria, Georgia, and Ukraine). The besieging of Ukraine, its heroic resistance, and the ensuing genocide have given the West a wake-up call.

The Russo-Ukrainian War, which belligerently began in 2014, must be won by the forces of freedom. In other words, it is paramount that Ukraine does not fall. As has been the case with most wars throughout history, it is never just about two contenders. The West must be determined to roll back Russian aggression. This can only be done by making it steadfastly clear that Russia's control over Ukraine will not be tolerated. Ironically, the side which has been losing the war is the one calling the shots. Through Putin's nuclear blackmail and the West's sheer cowardice, the U.S., EU, and NATO have grown to have a fear of fear itself, as Franklin Delano Roosevelt once remarked.

The fact that NATO is considerably more powerful than Russia goes unnoticed in Brussels. Expressed concerns of "escalation" and "provocation" have become the Biden administration's most common buzzwords. This genuflecting approach to resolving poignant international issues only serves freedom's enemies. The West is afraid that "crazy" Putin will press the nuclear finger if the West acts as it should and not according to his will. History, again, appears to have gone unlearned or is being ignored.

The post-WWII planet lived with two (later more) diametrically opposed superpowers possessing nuclear weapons. The most successful deterrent against an Armageddon was the notion of Mutually Assured Destruction (MAD). The understanding that a nuclear war would be catastrophic for all parties involved, prompted prudence and avoided a catastrophe. Neither the U.S. nor the U.S.S.R. ever renounced their willingness to use them. That is what assured its non-use. The first massive mistake the West has made since Putin invaded Ukraine is letting him have the monopoly of the nuclear verbiage. The rhetorical principle of MAD was violated by the U.S. and NATO. Words matter.

The unwillingness to formulate, early on, an NFZ over Ukrainian skies, has signaled to the aggressor the West's reluctance to defend the sovereignty of a strategic member of the democratic community. When Russian Foreign Minister Sergey Lavrov said that the free world will simply "get over" the Putin regime's invasion of Ukraine, he was reacting in adversarial coherence to the American and European reaction. The rationale opposing an NFZ is flawed.

Tobias Ellwood, a senior British Conservative MP who chairs the defense select committee, correctly critiqued his country's opposition to a Ukrainian NFZ as "misleading, simplistic and indeed defeatist to suggest engaging in a no-fly zone over Ukraine would automatically lead to a war, even nuclear conflict with Russia." Ellwood wisely added that the West should have "more confidence in managing these Cold War high-stakes scenarios." This is spot on.

The Biden administration has expressed a similar pattern of logic. WH Press Secretary Jen Psaki has repeatedly made the claim that an NFZ "would essentially mean the U.S. military would be shooting down planes, Russian planes." This fatalistic scenario adheres more to a political policy choice, in this case of backing down against Russian aggression, rather than actual military options. It is not sketched in stone that the Ukrainians themselves cannot be the material authors of, effectively, demilitarizing zones of the Ukrainian sky. With the proper military and technological hardware from the U.S. and NATO, Ukraine could disincentivize Putin's missiles and planes from flying over their country for purposes of war and genocide.

The idea of building a strategic missile defense shield over Europe, a project started in 2007 that was negligently scrapped in 2009 by Barack Obama in his "reset" appeasement rapprochement with the Russian dictator, was intended for such scenarios. Deterrence would have been served by such a system. Deterrence to the worst of war's ravages can still be avoided if the West man's up and decides it will not bear idly the execution of genocide and war crimes. Ukrainians can logistically carry out an NFZ mandate. This can be done from their territory or, if need be, from NATO or American bases. Belarusian territory has been enabling Putin's aggression from the beginning. Ukraine's allies must act in kind.

A group of 27 American foreign policy experts has penned an open letter calling for a limited NFZ. The list of weighty personalities includes Paula Dobriansky (former undersecretary of State for global affairs), Alexander Vershbow (former U.S. Ambassador to NATO and Russia), Ian Brzezinski (former deputy assistant secretary of defense), and Kurt Volker (former U.S. Ambassador to NATO). In the public missive, they state that "What we seek is the deployment of American and NATO aircraft not in search of confrontation with Russia but to avert and deter Russian bombardment that would result in massive loss of Ukrainian lives."

General Philip Breedlove, former Supreme Allied Commander in Europe and another signatory of the cited open letter to the Biden administration, noted that an NFZ could be conducted without the "bellicose rules of engagement." The former NATO top chief added: "How many casualties does it take before we take a different approach to this war?" The former commander of the Canadian military, General Rick Hillier, assessed the risk of not implementing an NFZ in Ukraine. "I know that NATO is a defensive organization, but you don't start defense at your front door," he said. Even former Defense Secretary Leon Panetta has acknowledged that "we ought to at least have that (NFZ) as a potential option."

Engaging in war successfully requires that all alternatives be on the table. Psychological warfare is a seminal piece in the military arsenal. When the Free World publicly announces that they will refrain from using certain weapons or refuse to apply strategies like an NFZ, they are following a loser's course. The sure path to defeat should not be accepted. Lieutenant Colonel Alexander Vindman called it well when he said, "There is no such thing as a risk-free option, at this point. There are only calibrated- and risk-informed options." Ukraine is democracy's battlefront today.

.

9 Is Russia Plotting a War Front in Latin America?

The Cuban, Venezuelan, and Nicaraguan dictatorships are probably more concerned than Washington and Brussels over the Kremlin's diatribes.

The Soviet Union's understanding of doctrinal internationalism split the world into regional spheres of influence, but with a caveat. The popular adage of the Brezhnev Doctrine's "what's mine is mine and what's yours is up for grabs" principle, was the cornerstone of Soviet foreign policy. It has been carried forward by the post-Soviet authoritarian regime of Vladimir Putin. Russia's blatant disregard for Ukrainian sovereignty and the civilized order of political relations is evidence of this. Recent declarations by high-ranking American military leaders and State Department officials have issued stark security warnings. Could Russia be plotting a Latin American, Ukraine-like, war front?

During a Senate Foreign Affairs Committee hearing on March 31, Deputy Assistant Secretary for Public Diplomacy, Policy, Planning, and Coordination, Kerri Hannan, testified about Russia's threat in the Western

Hemisphere. "The commitment to democracy in the Hemisphere has never seemed so urgent," Hannan stated and added that "while Russia tramples on Ukraine's democracy and threatens to export the Ukrainian crisis to the Americas, expanding its military cooperation with Cuba, Nicaragua and Venezuela." GOP Senator Marco Rubio (FL) concurred with the State Department official and said, "Russia is an acute problem, and it is a current challenge."

Hannan's testimonial declaration is not an isolated assessment. General Laura J. Richardson, the commander of the U.S. Southern Command, raised similar concerns on March 8 over Russian collusion with Latin American socialist dictatorships. Before members of the House Armed Services Committee, Richardson said that "Threats in South America, include transnational criminal organization as well as the meddling of both China and Russia." The four-star general highlighted to Congress that "Russia, a more immediate threat, is increasing its engagements in the hemisphere."

Yury Borisov, the Kremlin's deputy prime minister, said in January that he could "neither affirm nor exclude" whether

Russia would send military assets to Cuba or Venezuela. It is worth noting that days before the Russian invasion of Ukraine, Borisov paid a visit to Cuba, Venezuela, and Nicaragua. Dictator Putin has developed a close relationship with the tyrannical troika of Miguel Díaz-Canel, Nicolás Maduro, and Daniel Ortega. Russian state news agencies have made no secret of this alliance. Russian Foreign Minister Sergey Lavrov said in an address to the State Duma (Russia's figurative parliament) in January that "the three friendly countries agreed to consider ways to further deepen our strategic partnership in each and every field."

Putin's top diplomat simply stated an obvious fact. Except for an 8-year hiatus (1991-1999), Russia has maintained a tight bond with Latin American socialism. The former KGB officer, undoubtedly, revamped the post-totalitarian model from which he came. The mixture of a crony and state capitalist-driven economy, Putinism shares many key characteristics with the Sao Paulo Forum's dictatorial prototype, that concocted scheme devised by the deceased Cuban tyrant, Fidel Castro, in reaction to the fall of Soviet communism.

The Soviet Union invested heavily in promoting communism in the Americas. Putin's willingness to forgive $53 billion of Russian debt owed by the Castro-Communist dictatorship, reflects the understanding of a partnered relationship. Russia's activism in Latin America, following in the USSR's footsteps, is channeled through Castro's Cuba. The Russian GPS satellite spy base on the outskirts of Managua, the expansive military hardware transfer to Venezuela, and the espionage experimentation that, most likely, resulted in the Havana Syndrome in Cuba, all predate the invasion of Ukraine.

Putin may be seeking to scare the U.S.; threats of bringing the Russo-Ukrainian War into America's backyard could shed, however, surprising consequences for his regime, as well as Cuba, Venezuela, and Nicaragua. The people in those three captive nations could emulate the Ukrainians. A revolt is a possibility. If the Russian dictator arms and uses Cuban, Venezuelan, and Nicaraguan territory, they would be considered complicit war allies, like Belarus.

Such a scenario would prompt the West to extend sanctions against the three socialist regimes. Given the mixing of geography and national security, the U.S. and NATO would likely send war vessels to the Gulf of Mexico, the

Florida Straits, and the Caribbean Sea. Putin has proved to be a bumbling war strategist. The Cuban, Venezuelan, and Nicaraguan dictatorships are probably more concerned than Washington and Brussels over the Kremlin's diatribes. Ukraine may well be a key to freedom in Latin America.

10 The Ukrainian Killing Fields and the Radbruch Formula

The hideous massacres that Russia is committing and to which the world is a witness to, should suffice to energetically move the West and place potent offensive weapons in the hands of the Ukrainian armed forces.

Retreating Russian troops are leaving behind a trail of heinous atrocities. This was expected. Life, for the Putin regime and the country it controls, matters little. The Soviet Union and post-USSR Russia have a compelling history of waging war like savage barbarians. The liberated territories of Ukraine are showing the world that Russians have continued the uncivilized pattern of warfare that has characterized them for the last 105 years. The uncovered Ukrainian killing fields in Bucha, Irpin, Motyzhyn, Staryi Bykiv, Zabuchchya, Vorzel, Malaya Rohan, Trostyanets, and Mariupol raise a renewed international challenge to draw upon the Radbruch Formula against Russia in the International Criminal Court.

Ukraine's Foreign Minister Dmytro Kuleba called the horrific sightings, the "tip of the iceberg." Testimonial accounts, lamentably, abound. Four hundred twenty-one civilian casualties were uncovered on Sunday alone. Anatoly Fedoruk, the mayor of Bucha, a city on the outskirts of Kyiv that was under Russian occupation, noted that over two hundred eighty corpses were unearthed from mass graves. Photographs of dead civilians with their hands tied behind the back and gunshots to the head at close range offer clear signs of sadistic, execution-type killings. The naked dead bodies of women relay sessions of mass rape. Satellite images leave no room for doubt that the beastly crimes were committed by the Russian army.

Upon visiting Bucha on Monday, Ukrainian President Volodymyr Zelensky was visibly touched by the horror he was witnessing. Emphatically, he condemned this as an act of "genocide" and the execution of "war crimes." The Churchillian leader was not alone in this position. The U.S. view, as expressed by National Security Adviser Jake Sullivan, coincides with the Ukrainian authorities that highlight that this "show(s) further evidence of war crimes" against civilians. International outrage is leaving little room for timid reactions.

In a makeshift grave in a wooden area just outside Motyzhyn, a town 28 miles (ca. 45 kilometers) west of

Kyiv, the tortured bodies of Olha Sukhenko, her husband Ihor Sukhenko and their 25-year-old son, Oleksandr, were discovered by authorities. "They tortured and murdered the whole family of the village head," said Anton Herashchenko, former deputy minister at the Ukrainian Ministry of Internal Affairs. In addition to civilians and elected officials, Ukrainian prisoners of war (POW) offer further evidence of war crimes. On April 4, Ukrainian human rights ombudsman Lyudmyla Denisova confirmed that swapped prisoners of a recent exchange exhibited "signs of frostbitten limbs." The Ukrainian POW's, related Denisova, were imprisoned in basements without heating, denied food and kept without adequate clothing. Russia is unrelentingly violating the Geneva Conventions of 1949.

The Main Directorate of Intelligence of the Ukrainian Defense has made public a list with the names of Russian soldiers that operated in the Bucha locality during its occupation. The war crimes and the crimes against humanity committed rests on those soldiers, not only the Putin regime. Individual perpetrators bear responsibility The pathetic excuse of "just following orders" will not cut it. That matter was settled in 1946, thanks to the work of a German jurist, Gustav Radbruch, whose essay "Statutory

Lawlessness and Suprastatutory Law," outlined a course which judges in the Nuremberg Trials followed.

It was referred to as the "Radbruch Formula." As the Nazi regime collapsed, the liberating forces unveiled the horrors of National Socialism. It turned out that a whole legal structure validated the atrocities. True to military discipline, German commanders insisted that they were only "following orders." The Radbruch Formula established that if an act was so barbaric in nature, any law that authorized its execution was invalidated. Criminal accountability could not be pinned only on one person, in this case, Adolf Hitler. Individual culpability could not be circumvented.

U.S. President Abraham Lincoln issued, in 1863, the world's first modern codification of military conduct during a war. The "General Orders No. 100," (Lieber Code), with its 157 provisions, established the legal basis for civilized behavior in the conduction of war. Respect for civilian lives, gentlemanly composure by combatants, and a standardized treatment of POWs are some of the norms that Lincoln's war conduct codification sought to institute.

The invading Russian forces are proving that they are but a band of ghastly hordes. Putin's fabricated historical fable prescribes nothing less than genocide to wipe out Ukraine and Ukrainians. The hideous massacres that Russia is committing and to which the world is a witness to, should suffice to energetically move the West and place potent offensive weapons in the hands of the Ukrainian armed forces. The Free World can never say, they did not know or did not see.

11 Ukraine and the Revival of the West

The globalist world order that made China the world's factory and Russia the European Union's oil and gas provider is ethically anti-Western.

As Russia's war against Ukraine, with its ensuing genocide and flagrant war crimes' surpasses its first month, the West appears to be recovering from an identity crisis. Many Putin defenders in the Free World label the Ukrainian state as a "globalist" tool and look to the Russian despot as a force against "globalism." There is a grave contradiction in that reasoning. Ukraine and the principle of national sovereignty and democratic values may well turn out to be a needed revival for the West.

For semantic precision, the West is not about geography. It is a standard-bearer for a set of values that foster notions of consensual government, free societies, the rule of law, and natural rights. The antitheses to this social-political prototype, versions of totalitarian or authoritarian autocratic rule, have benefited enormously from the post-World War II order of a global commonwealth. This internationalist paradigm has been underlined by the premise that economic relations are primacy instigators of political conduct. China, Vietnam, the former USSR, Putin's Russia, and political actors like George Soros, have been prime beneficiaries of this model. This globalist paragon is anti-Western. This is the "globalism" that Putin apologists fail to see.

When good-intentioned Russian supporters argue that Ukraine is in the Eurasian country's "sphere of influence," they are trampling on the principles of self-governance and nationhood. While ironically, many of these Putin worshipers label themselves as "nationalists," they are negating the basis of a nation's right to exist territorially. In other words, they are perverting nationalism to fit a skewed historical and ideological narrative. One cannot be a nationalist in your country and believe that Ukraine and Ukrainians are not entitled to the same standards of sovereignty.

The globalist world order that made China the world's factory and Russia, the European Union's oil and gas provider, is ethically anti-Western. Despotic regimes like the Chinese and Russian have been prized winners of the "peace dividend" that followed the fall of Soviet communism. This view of a world order prioritized global commercial accommodations and believed that evildoers could be civilized by their financial entanglements with the West. The opposite has occurred. The non-democratic regimes in Russia and China have used their leverage against the Free World to advance their hegemonic objectives. The latter has been more furtive and asymmetrical. The former, not having the financial backup and being more time-constrained, resorted to more direct tactics.

Post-Soviet Russian armed aggression against other countries includes Moldova and Transnistria (1990-1992), Georgia (2008), Ukraine (2014-present) and Syria (2015-present). Through cyberwar, the Putin regime has attacked Estonia (2007), Lithuania (2008), Georgia (2008), Kyrgyzstan (2009), Kazakhstan (2009), Ukraine (2014-present), Germany (2015), and the U.S. (1996-present). Putin's Russia quickly rebuilt its relationship with communist Cuba, as well as established subversive partnerships with other socialist dictatorships in Venezuela and Nicaragua. Iran and its Hezbollah militias are de facto Russian foreign legion troops.

Ukraine, and its moral crusade against Russian tyranny, has opened the Free World's eyes and prodded its mind. The global scheme that has so empowered China and Russia is being revisited and potentially deconstructed. This is the best thing that could happen to the West. Ukrainian President Volodymyr Zelensky recently spoke (remotely) before the U.N. and correctly raised a moral dilemma for the international organization. Having an "aggressor and a source of war from blocking decisions about its own aggression," stated Zelensky when referring to Russia's permanent seat in the U.N.'s Security Council and its ability to veto any effective remedy, presents a structural contradiction that undermines the institution's mission. "If your current format is unalterable and there is simply no way out," he added, "then the only option would be to dissolve yourself altogether." The West has rediscovered its roots in Ukraine.

12 Christianity and a Divided West

As we observe Easter, the celebration of the resurrection of Jesus Christ, a greater trust in a transcendental order would help strengthen the values that have defined Western civilization.

Russia's invasion of Ukraine has made clear that there is a divide over the identity of the West and Western civilization. This has been especially palpable in the right and conservative circles. It has not, however, escaped the left entirely. As the world's largest religion celebrates its holiest week, it is worth noting and, perhaps, bridging the gaps of this division. The Free World (another name for the West) has come to the aid of a besieged Ukraine. For some, this sign of democratic solidarity has been too slow and not enough. For other Westerners, the aid should not have happened at all. Why is there a divide?

The West features a set of values, not geographically determined elements. Japan and South Korea are in Asia, yet they are part of the West. Those values include freedom, equality, justice, pluralism, rule of law, representative government, and open societies. Western civilization, the bedrock of the West, was built on a three-legged stool: Athens, Rome, and Jerusalem. Greek philosophy, Roman law, and Christian religion have been the hallmark of what constitutes being Western. When there is a disbalance within those three pillars, an identity crisis ensues.

Ukraine's heroic resistance has forced the Free World to rethink its role. So far, this has served to energize the West's essence. The Putin regime's outrageous invasion of Ukraine, undoubtedly, displayed a gross miscalculation of Western resolve to defend the principles of liberty and democracy. However, had the Free World preserved its compositional balance, preemptive actions by NATO, acting as the West's armed forces, could have dissuaded Russian tyranny from violating Ukrainian sovereignty and carrying out its current genocide campaign.

The Enlightenment brought with it many noble things. Among them was liberalism (both, classical and modern) and capitalism. However, not everything has proven to be of concrete support to republican institutions such as a free and virtuous citizenry, democratic government, and constitutional primacy. The Enlightenment represented a break with the past, the overrepresentation of individualism at the expense of the common interests, and an economic prototype that prioritized, over time, radical consumerism without considering national security issues or anthropological damage.

Classical and medieval notions of ordered liberty and traditional bonds were shattered. Thomas Hobbes' view of nature and Jean-Jacques Rousseau's prescription for remedying social ills laid the groundwork for totalitarian rule. Alexis de Tocqueville in *Democracy in America* (1835, 1840) keenly noted that such "democratization" trends were dangerous. By dissolving the relations which link people, like the family, religion, and the political community, a void develops that is filled by authoritarian rulers. An atomized, purposeless society, in other words, is the breeding ground for despots.

The American Revolution's success, when compared to the French as both are prototypes of a liberal political order, is due to the strong religious base that underpinned the U.S. founding and development. A virtuous society, a prerequisite for democratic rule, was bounded by a morality that religion shaped in America. Democracy works well in a morally fit society, which carefully balances rights and responsibilities. However, that Biblical foundation that gave the U.S. the advantage over other democratic experiments in the world, has been challenged with time's passage by radical secularism, socialism, and other atheistic tenets. In Europe, these dangerous patterns of political religions have had more success.

Ukraine's extraordinary ability to resist and roll back Russian aggression can be attributed to its moral reserves. The collective action of a determined people to be daring and heroic in acts of abnegation on behalf of their common identity, love of country, honor, family, and choosing death over bondage, all have factored into their survivorship. All these virtues draw upon classical and medieval thinking. The West has acted upon this boldness and has correctly armed the Ukrainians (although not nearly enough) and punished the Putin regime.

Some conservatives have been skeptical about supporting Ukraine. They point to toxic policies that many E.U. countries have adapted that get their intellectual premise from cultural Marxist doctrines of the Critical Theory series. While it is true that these political courses of Neo-Marxism undermine the very essence of democracy, Putin's Russia is not a viable alternative. When Alexander Dugin, the Russian dictator's ideological Rasputin, critiques Western "decadence," he does not differentiate between the vices of cultural Marxist policies (that deserve challenging), with noble Western standards of liberty, equality before the law, justice, and social compacts of consensual government.

As we observe Easter, the celebration of the resurrection of Jesus Christ, a greater reliance on a transcendental order would help strengthen the values that have defined Western civilization. Freedom, education, science, the value of life and the individual, all found advocates in Christianity. A post-liberal order is, simply, a liberal order that includes God. Happy Easter!

13 Is Ukraine Receiving Western Aid to Survive but Not Defeat Russia?

Ukraine must not just avoid a collapse. Russia must be defeated in the country they invaded.

Few people would have given Ukraine much hope on when the Russian invasion began. Surprisingly, over two months later, Europe's biggest landmass country is still free and sovereign. The world's second-largest army has been humiliated in the battlefield. The main objective: capturing Kyiv, killing President Volodymyr Zelenskyy, and installing another puppet government, has failed. Given these facts, many are wondering if Ukraine is receiving Western aid only in the amount and quality necessary to not collapse, but not enough to defeat Russia...

The Russian occupiers have lost 25% of their invading forces. Among the human losses, have been over 10 high-level Russian military commanders. Military experts concur that when this scenario unfolds, your troops are suffering defeat and forcing them closer to the front lines. There are many reasons one can give to explain the field superiority of the Ukrainians. Russia's army is stiff and follows a highly centralized military structure. The

Ukrainians, on the other hand, have brilliantly adopted Napoleonic strategies which exploits chaos and renders flexibility to field commanders. The numbers speak for themselves. Given this fact, why is the U.S. and NATO withholding their most advanced offensive weaponry?

American intelligence has been pivotal in partially explaining this epic Ukrainian success story. Logistics alone, however, will not suffice. On the military front, Ukraine has been requesting Patriot missiles, fighter jets, and smart offensive missiles to capitalize on Russia's vulnerabilities. This has not come about. Defensive weapons seem to be the thrust of the West's generosity. Wars are not won, however, limited to defensive infliction. It is a good thing that Ukrainian military commanders have been given autonomy in making military decisions in the field, instead of receiving instructions from Brussels or Washington.

The economic sanctions against the Putin regime have been spectacular. While it is true that these similar measures have no historic precedent, they are still insufficient. Since Russia invaded Ukraine, the West has transferred $66 billion in fossil fuel related purchases to the Russian dictator. This helps fund the Russian war machine. This finances the Russian genocide against the Ukrainian nation. The West's financial institutions have limited Putin's banks, but they have not derailed them totally. This leaves avenues that allow the evasion of the West's intention of denying Russia the resources to continue its aggression. Everyone knows what needs to be done. Since the Soviet days, the Eurasian country depends on oil and gas exports for their survivability. The U.S. and oil producing allies have the capability to replace the Russian market. Why isn't this happening?

If one accepts the argument that the West does not want the legitimate government of Ukraine to collapse, but it also does not want Russia to be defeated, the issue becomes a tragic paradox. One could make the argument that a prolonged war in Ukraine could bleed the Putin regime to death, resulting in its overthrow. Those that take this view are using Ukrainian lives and wealth for this purpose. Another position is that if Putin is defeated, the Russian dictator will go ballistic and make true on his nuclear blackmail. This defeatist position, which is antithetical to the West's Cold War strategy of Mutually Assured Destruction, casts aside the very nature of the victory of democracy and capitalism over Soviet communism.

The West must stop this piecemeal approach to aiding Ukraine. The immorality of using the Ukrainian people as pawns to crush the Putin regime goes against the values which Western civilization represents. The Ukrainian armed forces have already proved that they can defeat the Russian invaders. Since 2014, Ukraine has been preparing for a full-fledged Russian invasion. American and NATO military personnel knew that. They helped train the Ukrainians. Give them the weapons they need and starve the Russian war monster once and for all. Putin's off ramp will come quicker, the more his regime suffers. Ukraine must not just avoid a collapse. Russia must be defeated in the country they invaded.

14 American Policy Failures with Putin

Relations between democracies and dictatorships should be lukewarm at best, but never one of friendship, trust, or economic entanglement.

Republican and Democratic administrations have misread Vladimir Putin's kleptocratic regime. The West, in general, has diagrammed policy towards post-Soviet Russia under false perceptions. Sun Tzu's notion that, "If you know yourself but not the enemy, for every victory gained you will also suffer a defeat," (*The Art of War*) has epitomized the Free World's course following the collapse of the USSR.

The fall of Soviet communism produced a euphoria in the West. Rightly so. The wholesale theft of Eastern and Central Europe by the Soviet Union following World War II, the ascent of Chinese communism, and the invasion of South Korea by the North, prompted a comprehensive Western reaction to challenge the malignancy of communism. Why did the West assume Russia would transition into a democracy?

George H.W. Bush and Bill Clinton inherited the dividend of the Reagan Doctrine. Capitalism, as the West's premier socioeconomic model, played an important role in sinking socialism. However, it was not the only factor. The morality inherent in Western values were paramount instruments. Ideology mattered. America and the international liberal order that emerged after the defeat of National Socialism in Europe was not just about economics.

The transition following the breakup of the Soviet Union contained suspicious elements from the beginning. The 1990s in Russia witnessed the biggest privatization program in history. The massive transfer of state-owned enterprises (SOE) into private hands proved to be a deceitful ploy. It was legalized theft. The managers of those very SOEs ended up "selling" to themselves these assets. With state subsidized credit, regulated low prices, shares and voucher schemes, a newly formed oligarchic class with political ties to power and the Soviet past was consolidated. Elections lost their competitiveness, as the kleptocracy rigged the political system.

Under these conditions, Clinton signed the 1994 Budapest Memorandum which made the U.S. a guarantor of

Ukraine's sovereignty, in exchange for the surrender of their nuclear arsenal, then the world's third largest. How could Clinton trust Russia? After all, it was clear by then that Boris Yeltsin had done a superb job in dismantling the USSR, but a feeble one in establishing a democracy.

The Islamic attacks of September 11 lead George W Bush to see Putin as an ally. He went so far as to publicly say in 2001 that he had seen Putin's soul and was convinced of his honesty. One wonders if Russia's invasion of Georgia in 2008 changed Bush's mind. Judging from the West's reaction to this brutal aggression, Putin continued to be a stealth thug.

Barack Obama was, by far, the biggest dupe for the Putin regime. The actions of his two presidential terms empowered the Russian dictator in unprecedented ways. The dismantling of the nascent Europe defensive missile system, denying arms sales to Ukraine and torpedoing its NATO entry, authorizing American uranium access rights, and a "red-line" invitation in Syria, were all overtures to Putin for a failed "reset" policy. In the 2012 elections, as Obama debated, Mitt Romney, he ridiculed the Republican candidate for suggesting Putin was a threat to the West. The

Obama Doctrine turned out to be an appeasement treatise that galvanized Russian adventurism.

Putin's invasion of Ukraine in 2014 was met with weakness and moral ambivalence by Obama. This validated Russia's blatant claim that, in some absurd manner, it had a sphere of influence "right" to pulverize Ukrainian sovereignty. At that moment, the Western international liberal order that was built after the Second World War, was formally buried. Russian cyber-attacks, the election meddling, and the Havana Syndrome, were only some manifestations of Putin's imperialist endeavors that would follow.

Donald Trump, despite some of his reckless public statements, was the president who caused the most damage to the Putin regime. The bombings in Syria that killed Russian soldiers and arms sales to Ukraine, along with the training of its military, directly challenged Russian dictatorial interests. However, it was the remarkable increase in American oil production that most hurt Putin's war machine.

Fossil-fuel sales revenues, as was the case with the USSR, remains Russia's key to hard currency entry. Collapsing oil prices, resulting from the increase in supply under Trump's watch, was a financial blow to the Eurasian kleptocracy. Coincidently, this was part of Reagan's strategy to rollback Soviet communism. Words and symbols, however, are vital in politics. Trump erred by stubbornly refusing to address Putin as a dictator. This played into the Left's narrative. It also helped Putin.

The 2022 Russian invasion of Ukraine has opened a new chapter in American and European foreign policy. The West must partner with the free exclusively.

15 Memorial Day, the Nixon Doctrine and Ukraine

The brave Ukrainian nation has proved that the Nixon Doctrine, which Reagan strengthened and proved feasible, can work in the 21st century.

Memorial Day honors American fallen soldiers who died in war. It was formerly known as Decoration Day, as it was a marked occasion to visit the war dead's graves and decorate them with flags and other patriotic ornaments. Whether one accepts it or not, Providence has anointed America with certain qualities and tasks. It's role in the modern world cannot be overlooked or denied. The U.S. is the bulwark of Western civilization and values.

The two world wars bore a cost of over 522,000 American lives. This price tag for freedom is never cheap. American soldiers have paid it time and time again. The post-World War II order greatly advantaged Soviet expansionism. The Truman Doctrine, a foreign policy course designed to contain communist imperialism, was the established U.S. norm for 34 years (1947-1981). Korea, Western Europe, Latin America, the Middle East, and Southeast Asia were all conflict theaters where this defensive blueprint was implemented.

 Believing Marxism-Leninism in political power could be defeated, Ronald Reagan replaced the Truman Doctrine with a multifaceted offensive approach. The Reagan Doctrine (1981-1989) structural sought to rollback communism, not just limit its spread. Reagan's methodological plan worked. The demise of Soviet communism, which had battlefields in Latin America, Afghanistan, Africa, Eastern Europe, Middle East, and Asia, can be attributed to this foreign policy course.

The loss of American lives was minimal during this offensive crusade on behalf of international freedom. In part, the Reagan Doctrine adopted and perfected an earlier U.S. foreign policy strategy, the Nixon Doctrine (1969-1975). As American popular opinion soured on the Vietnam War, Richard Nixon, who inherited a noble war run badly by previous Democratic administrations, shifted to the "Vietnamization" of the conflict. The Nixon Doctrine called for the support of allies by training, arming, offering them logistical support and systemic assurances, but not directly involving American combat troops in the effort.

The conclusion of U.S. involvement in the Vietnam War, did not mean that the war by the communist North on the non-communist South, had ended. The Nixon Doctrine was the bedrock of South Vietnam's survival, while avoiding further American casualties. The 94th Congress (1975-1977), under Democratic control, betrayed America's commitment to South Vietnam by cutting military aid to the U.S. ally and former war partner, despite the vehement request by then president, Gerald Ford. The Nixon Doctrine was incinerated, and consequently, Saigon fell.

Reagan made sure that that its adaptation of Nixon's premise that called for the supporting of freedom fighters and friendly governments was credible. Thus, the Nicaraguan resistance, the Afghan freedom forces, the Angolan UNITA fighters, the government of El Salvador, and opposition movements throughout the Socialist bloc in Europe, were some of the recipients of American determination to combat communism. This coherent foreign policy allowed the Free World to defeat Soviet

Marxist rule and hegemony, with a minimal shedding of American life.

Today, Ukraine offers the West an opportunity to defeat global expansive tyranny, without shedding American lives. On February 24, Putin's second invasion of Ukraine (the first was in 2014), destroyed the illusion that post-Soviet Russia was somehow transformed for the better by the reconfiguration of its economy. The former KGB dictator has used the global capitalist system to build a kleptocracy that is directly challenging the international rule of law-based order, the West naively believed existed.

Joe Biden confused Ukraine's Volodymyr Zelensky with Afghanistan's Ashraf Ghani. The Ukrainian president's call for ammunition and not an Uber airlift. The West must increase its weapons commit to Ukraine so that it can win. This would be the perfection of the Nixon Doctrine, whose functional mission was to safeguard freedom, while avoiding American war casualties.

Ukraine is today the battlefield where the forces of democracy are fighting autocratic imperialism. The good side is winning. Not one shed of American, or NATO soldier's blood has been spilled. The brave Ukrainian nation has proved that the Nixon Doctrine, which Reagan strengthened and proved feasible, can work in the 21st century.

On Memorial Day, as we honor America's fallen on behalf of liberty, the Ukrainian people, armed forces, and civilian militias, must also be remembered and supplied with the necessary weaponry. If the Free World does not do this, at some point American and NATO soldiers may have to confront Russian aggression. Let us honor and salute the brave soldiers who today are defending freedom, wherever they are.

About the Author

Julio M. Shiling is a political scientist, author, lecturer, media commentator, columnist, and director of the political forums and digital publications Patria de Martí and The CubanAmerican Voice. He holds a master's degree in political science from Florida International University (FIU) in Miami, Florida, and is a member of The American Political Science Association and the PEN Club of Cuban Writers in Exile.

He is the author of fourteen books, including the much-acclaimed *Dictatorships and Their Paradigms: Why Do Some Dictatorships Fall and Others Do Not?* (2013, 2022), formerly a two-volume work and now formatted into one book. Being fluent in Spanish has allowed him to publish his works in that language as well. His articles and essays have been reproduced in dozens of print and electronic publications in the United States, Latin America, and Europe. As a political scientist and media commentator, he is a frequent guest on local, national, and international television, radio, podcast, and other media platform programs.

Since 2006, Julio M. Shiling has directed Patria de Martí. In 2020, he launched The CubanAmerican Voice, a digital media platform in English. Patria de Martí was awarded the 2015 Human Rights Freedom Award by the Asociación por la Paz Continental (ASOPAZCO), a Spanish NGO dedicated to the promotion of human rights in the world. Additionally, in 2015, he was conferred the Cuban Flag recognition in Boston, Massachusetts, on the celebration of the Grito de Yara. In 2017, he received the Herencia Award from Cuban Cultural Heritage, for his contribution to Cuban culture. He has also founded and managed insurance and financial services companies.

As a lecturer, he regularly participates in forums, conferences, panel discussions, and other public speaking gatherings. In addition, Patria de Martí sponsors "Symposiums for a Free World," a series of conferences designed to promote greater civic awareness bonded to freedom and democracy.

Born in Havana, Cuba, he went into exile with his family at the age of six. After a brief stay in Madrid, Spain, they relocated to the United States, settling in Union City and West New York, both cities in the state of New Jersey. A few years later, they moved to Miami, Florida, where he currently resides.